Prophetic Prayer to Sonship

by
David P. Ward

Unless otherwise indicated, all Scripture quotations are taken from the *King James Version* of the Bible.

Prophetic Prayer to Sonship
ISBN 0-88144-220-8
Copyright © 2004 by
David P. Ward
New Creation Missions International
P. O. Box 596
Wagoner, Oklahoma 74467

(918) 733-9900
www.ncmidave.com

Published by
Christian Publishing Services
P. O. Box 701434
Tulsa, Oklahoma 74170

Printed in the United States of America. All rights reserved under International Copyright Law. Contents and/or cover may not be reproduced in whole or in part in any form without the express written consent of the Publisher.

Contents

Introduction	Four Words for "Prayer"	5
Chapter One	*Proseuche* — The Call to Prayer	7
Chapter Two	*Deomai* — Supplicating in the Spirit	19
Chapter Three	Do All Things Work Together for Good?	33
Chapter Four	*Entunchano* — The Power of Intercession	41
Chapter Five	*Aiteo* — Placing a Demand on the Covenant	51
Chapter Six	What Time Is It?	69
A Sinner's Prayer		75

Introduction

Four Words for "Prayer"

We are about to begin an exciting journey on the arena of prayer! I encourage you to open up your heart and mind to the Holy Spirit. Make a decision right now to have a meek (teachable) spirit and to be a student of the Word of God, ready to go places in thought and revelation where you have never been before.

The Greek (Koine) language has over seven thousand more words in it that are used than does the English language. There are four words in the Greek language for our word "love." There are several words in the Greek language for our word "power." In the Greek language there are four words for our English word "prayer." In this book, we will major on the various types of prayer.

The original New Testament was written in Koine Greek, *Koine* meaning "common." This study on these Greek words is by no means an exhaustive study, but I believe it will help you in developing your understanding on the power of prayer and open your mind to the different types of prayer that are available to you as a Spirit-filled Christian.

The original form of the Old Testament was written in Hebrew. It is absolutely a fascinating study to examine the word "prayer" in the New Testament. The four Greek words for "prayer" used in this book are *proseuche, deomai, entunchano,* and *aiteo.*

Proseuche - English word: Pray. A two-way conversation with God. Communion and fellowship with intense meaning and fulfillment.

Deomai - English word: Supplicate. To stand in the gap for others in prayer that, based upon their lifestyle, do not seem to deserve our prayers. Also, this type of prayer can be used for those in authority over us.

Entunchano - English word: Intercession. The art of prayer to stand in the gap for a person, a group of people, or an entire nation. The Holy Spirit prays through your spirit (Romans 8:26-27).

Aiteo - English word: Ask. To place a loving demand on the covenant, based upon relationship.

I believe these Greek words will come alive in you as you read this book, *Prophetic Prayer to Sonship,* and they will assist you in going to a deeper and higher realm of prayer.

David P. Ward

Chapter One

PROSEUCHE — THE CALL TO PRAYER

The Greek word for prayer which we will study in this chapter is *proseuche,* meaning "a two-way conversation with God, communion, and fellowship with intense meaning and fulfillment."

First Thessalonians 5:16 says, **"Rejoice evermore."** This scripture is telling us to rejoice evermore. How many times have you tried to rejoice evermore? You might be thinking, *That might have been easy for Paul to say, but he didn't have to live with my husband.* Or you might have thought, *Paul could say that because he was an apostle.* Sometimes we think about prayer so religiously. My assignment is to help illuminate your thinking in the power of prayer.

First Thessalonians 5:17 says, **"Pray without ceasing."** Not only does Paul tell us to rejoice evermore, but then he has the audacity to say, **"Pray without ceasing."** The word "pray" in this verse in the Greek is *proseuche.* Paul tells us to be in communion with God without ceasing. How can we do that? How is it that we can be in communion with God while driving down the road, taking the kids to school, washing the dishes, or working a full-time job?

God's Not Into a Rigid Prayer Structure

I was in a denominational church that put a tremendous structure to prayer. We always had an attitude that we had to pray or something bad could happen to us. Prayer was a drudgery because there was so much demand upon our time.

In the first church I pastored years ago, there was a lady who got mad at me because I would pray with my eyes open in church during my prayers. She said, "Pastor, you're supposed to pray with your eyes closed!"

Some people think the only way to pray is on your knees. Others believe you have to reverently fold your hands and change your voice to Elizabethan English: "Thou gracious heavenly Father from whence thou hast given me grace to see thee."

Even in Full Gospel circles, we prayed religiously, yet we never saw anything supernatural happen. I experienced the historical Jesus, but not the living Jesus. I heard countless sermons on what the Lord had done historically, and we prayed and "hoped for the best" that maybe somehow we could get through to the throne of God.

I remember the "prayer stance" we would get in when it was time to pray. We would grab the wooden chair, turn it backwards, get down on one knee and grab the back of the chair intently. The preacher would get this awful look on his face – like folks do when they are jogging – and begin to pray. The people prayed and breathed at the same time!

The Role of "Listening" in *Proseuche*

Proseuche with God is more than turning colors and praying in Elizabethan English. The power of learning to commune with God is to listen when He speaks. This is what He intends for His people to do, whether they are doing the dishes or driving down the highway.

What did Jesus have to say about *proseuche?* There is a call to prayer, a place where we can commune with God, and He desires that we hear His voice.

Luke 9:1 says, **"Then he [Jesus] called his twelve disciples together, and gave them power and authority over all devils, and to cure diseases."**

I remember that many times I would pray enough just to ease my conscience. Do you ever remember lying down on your bed and praying, "God, bless Mom, Dad, Tom, Val, Sue, Lauren, and Michael"? After you went through all of your brothers and sisters, you fell asleep! My prayer life was, "Lord, I've got to get all of this in because I know it is the right thing to do." That's why a lot of people go to church, because "it's the right thing to do."

You can even go to an anointed church just enough where you feel the presence of God, hear a good word, and pray when you feel you need to. That is not how to live in victory! That is not what *proseuche* is all about. The Bible says, **"The just shall live by faith . . ."** (Habakkuk 2:4; Romans 1:17; Galatians 3:11; and Hebrews 10:38). The Bible tells us to commune with God without ceasing.

Dunamis (Power)

Now, let's look at Luke 9:1 again. **"Then he called his twelve disciples together, and gave them power and authority over all devils, and to cure diseases."**

There are five Greek words for the word "power." This word "power" in Luke 9:1 means inherent power or power that is stored up within. We get our word "dynamo" or "dynamite" from this word. This word power is *dunamis*.

I like to think of *dunamis* as being like a laundry detergent. There's something about those grains of detergent that when water hits those granules, all kinds of cleansing strength is released to cut through the dirt, grime, and grease. When those little dynamos are energized, what is built within is manifest.

Exousia (Delegated Authority)

The word "authority" comes from the Greek word *exousia,* which means delegated authority, the ability to engage or to enforce. Jesus gave His disciples the very ability of His Father. It was stored up within them and could be released to enforce Satan's defeat at the name of Jesus! This is the kind of authority the Father wants us to walk in as prophetic people.

The Prophetic Church

The greatest harvest, the greatest revival, that this world has ever seen is unfolding in the earth today. This prophetic movement of people will know the heart of

God. They will know what is the mind (plan) of the Spirit (Romans 8:27). The former and latter rain will culminate the last two centuries of what we have learned to a greater level of understanding concerning our prayer lives. We don't have to pray. *We get to pray!*

We are growing from glory to glory. You will see an anointing that will rest on the people of God who answer the call of prayer. A spirit of prayer will rise up to go to deeper streams that will hear with accuracy the Father's agenda for His Church today. Billye Brim calls the last day Church the "glorious Church." The late Dr. Lester Sumrall called it the "militant Church." The late Kenneth E. Hagin spoke of the "triumphant Church." I call it the "prophetic Church." It involves the same group of people.

In the glorious Church, the fivefold ministries will work together without fear or competition; without wondering who is going to "hold the money." The prophetic Church will not have "money concerns" or "money problems."

It is time for the Church to walk without being threatened by one another, where the apostle and prophet can flow with the pastor, teacher, and evangelist. No one will be insecure, because they will know who they are. This type of local church is where the pastor doesn't have to spend all of his time pacifying the people. He teaches them the Word and they will begin to grow.

In the next few years, we are going to see an attitude toward prayer change drastically. Many churches today are lackadaisical, and when you talk about intercessory prayer on a week night, usually two or three people show up. Jesus said, **"My house shall be called the house of prayer** *[proseuche]* **..."** (Matthew 21:13).

Jesus' Example in *Proseuche* Prayer

Luke 9:18 states, **"And it came to pass, as he was alone praying, his disciples were with him...."** The Head of the Church was alone praying and His disciples were with Him. How can you be alone praying and people be with you? When you are in *proseuche!*

- "Oh, I don't have time for prayer. My husband, he's ugly!"
- "I don't have time to pray. I've got the kids!"
- "The only rest I get is a few hours at night, and you want me to pray?"
- "How can I pray without ceasing?"

The Church world taught us that we had to fold our hands, pray on our knees with our eyes shut, and look like we were in pain when we prayed. Get a revelation on prayer! You can pray when you are doing dishes, on your job, or tending to your kids, and you can pray with your eyes open!

Jesus was alone *(proseuche)* with God, and His disciples were with Him. He had some awesome conversations with His Father. He received the Father's agenda and enjoyed time with Him. It must have been exciting, because the disciples took notice of Jesus in *proseuche* with His Father.

In Luke 18:11-14 Jesus was saying, "When you pray *(proseuche)*, don't carry on like the Pharisees." Jesus said to tune everyone out and listen. Get in the secret place of the Most High. You can be with people and still be alone praying.

Let's look at Luke, chapter 11. Verse 1 says, **"And it came to pass, that, as he was praying** *[proseuche]* **in a certain place, when he ceased, one of his disciples said unto him, Lord, teach us to pray** *[proseuche]***. . . ."** The disciples must have seen a tremendous joy and release come over Jesus in those prayer vigils. They wanted to hear and experience what Jesus was doing in that secret place. Jesus was totally enveloped in the Father's presence.

Jesus could have been on His knees or walking, but the Scriptures say He was in a certain place, alone with God, and His disciples were with Him. "Lord, teach us to commune. . . ." So many times we have heard from our spiritual leaders, "You need to pray," but how many of them have really told us "how" to pray?

How many times were we told, "You just need to read your Bible." We have to teach people how to study the Bible, not just read the Bible. We need to learn to tap into revelation knowledge where the Holy Spirit can illuminate the Scriptures to us. That's where sitting under anointed teachers is so vital in the hour in which we are living.

Jesus said, **He that hath seen me hath seen the Father . . ."** (John 14:9). Then He said, **"For he shall not speak of himself; but whatsoever he shall hear, that shall he speak . . ."** (John 16:13). How could He say that? Because of the time He spent in communion with our heavenly Father.

How could Paul say, **"Be followers together of me . . ."** (Philippians 3:17)? How is it that Jesus knew what to say and when to say it? At times He would be quiet in front of religious or political men, and at other times He would speak up boldly! Jesus told the scribes and Pharisees, **"Ye are like unto whited sepulchres,** which indeed appear beautiful outward, but are within full of dead men's bones, and of all uncleanness"** (Matthew 23:27). That was pretty bold to say to the religious leaders of His day.

Sometimes I believe there should be a Holy Ghost boldness to speak up to some religious leaders today in that same spirit of faith. This anointing came because of spending time listening, communing, and fellowshipping with our heavenly Father.

Doctrine or Spiritual Sensitivity?

Many ministers today are judged on their doctorate of divinity instead of their spiritual sensitivity. I've heard ministers who were highly educated beyond their own intelligence.

Smith Wigglesworth never graduated from high school. Yet he had power to raise the dead. Who would you rather have pray for you when cancer attacks your body? The minister with the Ph.D. (that's knowledge piled high and deep) or the minister who can touch the throne of God? (In other words, ministers led by their intellect rather than by the Spirit. God is not against education, but the intellect must be in submission to the Spirit of God.)

Proseuche Begins with Praise and Worship

Pastors want their congregations to rejoice evermore and pray without ceasing, but nobody knows how to do it. Jesus gave us the steps to *proseuche* in Luke 11. I believe the disciples said, "Lord, there is something going on with You and the Father and we want to do that." So Jesus responded, "This is how you do it. **'Our Father which art in heaven, Hallowed be thy name'**" (Luke 11:2).

Jesus said to begin to praise Him. Begin to thank Him for His goodness and mercy. Begin to worship the Lord for His mercy. Exalt Him in your heart, mind, and body. There is something about lifting your voice and operating in authority with a heart filled with praise that penetrates the throne of God.

Wigglesworth said that the Lord will move over a thousand people to get to one who is moving in faith. We need to learn to channel that inherent power inside of us that we received when we were born again. You might say, "Well, I don't feel that power inside of me when I pray. I don't feel I have any authority over these bad circumstances."

Rising Up in Your Spiritual Authority

In Second Timothy 1:7 Paul said, **"For God hath not given us a spirit of fear; but of power, and of love** [agape]**, and of a sound mind."** There is a spirit of authority within you that can rise up in an attitude of victory, causing you to know that your prayers avail much. You have authority, love, and a sound mind.

There are three areas where Satan hits the young believer:

- He wants you to stay ignorant to the authority that you have in the name of Jesus.
- Satan wants to keep you upset and offended all the time so you will continually harbor bitterness

and unforgiveness. Then, your prayers *(proseuche)* will be hindered.

- He wants your mind to think there is no use to pray because God never seems to answer your prayers anyway. Satan wants to keep you as a believer in a state of confusion so that your faith cannot operate.

The devil doesn't want you to know who you are in Christ. He wants to keep you jealous and frustrated when someone else gets their answer to prayer and you don't. If Satan can keep you out of the love walk and in unforgiveness, your faith won't work.

We always quote Mark 11:23-24 about having the God-kind of faith working in us, but we leave off the next verse about forgiveness. Jesus said in verse 25, **"And when ye stand praying** *[proseuche]*, **forgive. . . ."** Start out praising and worshipping the Lord. Then, begin to move over into communion with God.

Jesus went on to pray, **"Thy kingdom come . . ."** (Luke 11:2). We need to realize that the Kingdom of God is within us, but the agenda of God must be birthed into the earth through men and women. We are to triumph over the works of the devil. We are to lift our voices and proclaim the Word of God boldly from our lips.

Every day make the pronouncement, **"Thy kingdom come. Thy will be done, as in heaven, so in earth"** (Luke 11:2). The Kingdom of God is righteousness, peace, and joy in the Holy Ghost. What is loosed in heaven, you can loose on the earth. When we have the heart of God flowing through our voices, proclaiming His will, our prayers *(proseuche)* will avail much (James 5:16).

If you are in lack, you can say, "Thy Kingdom come. Prosperity, be released." If you are sick, you can say, "Thy Kingdom come. Health is mine!" Every Christian wants to receive the blessings of God, but not every Christian wants to learn how to pray with power and authority.

Brother Kenneth E. Hagin used to say that there is a big difference between head faith and heart faith. I believe that heart faith is released when we have had communion *(proseuche)* with God. When I proclaim the Kingdom of God, I say, "I am the righteousness of God in Christ."

The anointing to pray comes when we are in fellowship and communion with the Lord. This is how we develop a spirit of prayer.

Chapter Two

DEOMAI — SUPPLICATING IN THE SPIRIT

We are now going to further our study in Koine Greek and analyze the word *deomai*, which means "to stand in the gap for others in prayer that, based upon their lifestyles, do not seem to deserve our prayers." This type of prayer can be used for spiritual and natural authority alike.

First Timothy 2:1 says, **"I exhort therefore, that, first of all, supplications, prayers, intercessions, and giving of thanks, be made for all men."** In other words, supplicate for those in authority.

Supplicating for Government Leaders

We have to supplicate *(deomai)* for our governmental leaders and our spiritual leaders. This word "supplicate" comes from the Greek word *deomai,* which means "to stand in the gap for someone, even if we think they don't deserve it." Supplication is not based on whether you like the person or not. That is why we are to stand in the gap and pray for our governmental leaders. Regardless of our political party, we are to earnestly pray for those who are in office, **"that we may lead a quiet and peaceable life . . ."** (1 Timothy 2:2).

Great things can happen if we will get our prayer assignments from the Holy Spirit and pray out His plans for kings and presidents.

Have you ever thought about our president needing us to supplicate for him on a daily basis? For example, it is paramount that our president lead us as a nation to bless and stand with the nation of Israel. The Bible is clear that if we are on Israel's side, then we are on the Lord's side. We must undergird our president so he will make the right decisions in blessing Israel in every capacity.

Supplicating for Spiritual Leaders

Supplicating is also very important concerning praying for our pastors. Some folks change churches almost as often as they change cars! What we need to realize is that the imperfectness of a pastor does not mean that he is not called of God. The Bible tells us as Christians, **"God set [strategically positioned] the members every one of them in the body, as it hath pleased him"** (1 Corinthians 12:18).

Isn't that amazing? The Lord doesn't ask you where you want to go to church. I remember someone came up with the billboard, "Go to the church of your choice." Actually, if you are listening, the Holy Spirit might be telling you to hook up with a church that is fifty miles away from where you live. Can you believe that? How inconvenient can you get, having to drive an hour to church? We have people in our congregation who have been driving thirty to fifty miles one way for over four years. Hearing the prophetic voice of God is not always going to be the easiest, but the rewards are "out of this world"!

"Well, I'm not going back to that church anyhow because the pastor walked right by me and didn't speak." Or maybe you've heard the statement, "I'm not going back because I didn't feel the anointing on the pastor's message he delivered Sunday morning." This is when we know it is time to come out of the spiritual nursery and let someone else have a chance at the bottle!

There is a time to move out of a church, and that is when the Holy Spirit leads you to do so. But it is always after much prayer. It is always after you have spent much time in supplication *(deomai)* for your spiritual leader. If your pastor is preaching the uncompromised Word of God and if you are in a church where you can say that you are being spiritually fed, then to fall out over an offense is not the Lord's will. Continue to supplicate for him.

It is good to know that when we are going through adversity or when tribulation comes, we know that we know we have been strategically positioned by God to be in the local church. You know who your pastor is and where you belong because you have been in *proseuche* with God and have supplicated for your spiritual leader.

Sometimes when you go into prayer, you begin to listen to that still small voice and the Holy Spirit begins to search inside and direction comes. You might not always like what you are hearing or what He is leading you to do. Our feelings can fool us. We can't afford to go by feelings when it comes to prayer and listening to that still small voice. The awesome thing about the Spirit of

God is, just because you would rather ignore what He wants you to deal with doesn't mean that He will ignore it!

The commitment that you will need in these last days to come into sonship, to come into a developed prayer life, the commitment to your pastor and to your local church, cannot be based upon feelings or emotions. Just because you might go through what the Apostle Peter called "suffering in the flesh" does not mean that finding the will of God is always going to be an easy venture.

After being involved with Charismatics for over thirty years, I know it is possible to find some well-meaning believer to prophesy something that you are wanting to hear. It's just like taking the Bible and making it say what you want it to say. The devil and his cohorts don't have to listen to your private interpretation of the Bible.

Deomai Based Upon God's Word

Your prayer life must be based upon the Word of God. Reading good books concerning prayer and the Spirit-filled life, coupled with sitting under an anointed pastor, will go a long way in causing you to grow up **"unto a perfect [mature] man, unto the measure of the stature of the fulness of Christ"** (Ephesians 4:13).

Sometimes suffering in the flesh in doing the will of God can be very uncomfortable on our flesh and even downright painful. That's why Paul told Timothy, **"Endure hardness, as a good soldier of Jesus Christ"** (2 Timothy 2:3).

There is a strength in *proseuche* to carry out the will of God in your life. When your prayers don't feel like they are reaching the ceiling or when you feel like quitting, there is an anointing to break the yoke of discouragement.

First Timothy 2:1 says, **"First of all, supplications** *[deomai]*, **prayers** *[proseuche]*, **intercessions** *[entunchano]*, **and giving of thanks, be made for all men."**

Waiting Upon the Lord

When we come into a public assembly (this is what Timothy was referring to in this verse), we need to learn to wait upon the Lord. Brother Kenneth E. Hagin told many stories about being in church where you could hear a pin drop and not one baby would even cry because everyone was under a holy presence. They were caught up in an atmosphere of prayer.

We will see the prophetic church return to meetings like this before the Lord's return. It's actually already happening in churches where the pastor and the people are hungry for a move of God. Prophetic prayer comes because of a conducive atmosphere where the Holy Spirit is allowed to move.

The old Pentecostal pioneers of the last century in the early 1900s knew the power of waiting upon the Lord. The Azusa Street Revival didn't just happen. It was birthed by people who knew how to pray and then wait upon the Lord.

Travailing in Prayer

Prophetic prayer that brings us to intercession is compared to the birth pains of childbearing. The Prophet Isaiah knew what it was to be impregnated with the heart of God. The Apostle Paul knew that there was a vein of intercessory prayer he called "travailing" in Galatians 4:19: **"My little children, of whom I travail in birth again until Christ be formed in you."**

What does a man know about travail and having birth pains? Very little, I'm sure, unless he understands the travail one goes through when he is impregnated with what the old Pentecostals called "a burden to pray." There are times when you are carrying something in your spirit that can only come through with this type of prayer.

If you have never heard of travailing in intercession, I ask you to keep a teachable spirit and to be open to the Holy Spirit to take you into a realm of prayer where so many results can come when we learn to yield to the spirit of intercession and travail.

Remember, **"The carnal mind is enmity against God . . ."** (Romans 8:7). Paul said, **"But we have the mind of Christ"** (1 Corinthians 2:16). The carnal mind is always against what it does not understand. Sonship requires us to move into the arena of faith which comes through sensitivity of heart and a meek (teachable) spirit.

Those who have birthed any move of God in the earth know the power of travailing in the Spirit through intercession and are willing to pray until they "pray through." Romans 8:26 states:

> **Likewise the Spirit also helpeth** [takes hold together with] **our infirmities** [the limitations that our five physical senses bring]: **for we know not what we should pray** *[proseuche]* **for as we ought: but the Spirit itself** [Himself] **maketh intercession** *[entuchano]* **for us with**

groanings [travail] **which cannot be uttered** [in articulate speech].

First of all, the Holy Spirit is not an "it." The Holy Spirit is a real being and is not in neutered form. The Holy Spirit can be grieved (Ephesians 4:30).

For years Vonda and I have had an old upright piano. Since the time we were married, we have carried this monstrous piano with us across the country. I remember one time we leased a nice apartment that was on the second floor. We wondered why we forgot about the piano. It was a task getting the piano up those stairs. There was no way I was going to pick that upright piano up by myself. Not even Vonda and my boys (who were little at the time) could have carried that piano up those stairs. I had to get some big, strong men to move it. They "took hold together with me" to move that piano. Without their help, we would have made a futile attempt because I was physically limited as to what I could do as one man.

This is what the Holy Spirit comes to do when we are praying out something we are carrying in our hearts. He takes hold together with us and aids us in getting the job done through intercessory prayer. It's amazing! Paul even said that sometimes our minds are limited in knowing exactly what to pray *(proseuche)* for, so the Holy Spirit moves over us in a spirit of prayer and helps us pray out even with groanings from deep within that sometimes aren't even in the form of words.

You haven't lived as a Christian until you get a burden to pray for a child in the middle of the night when the Spirit of God wakes you up. Suddenly, you know there is a baby in danger. You know it deep inside of you. You just know it. It might be hours, days, weeks, or months before you find out who you were praying for.

And you might never find out who you were praying for until you get to heaven.

But oh, what a joy it is when you are allowed to see or hear the results of your praying through! Can you imagine where the Church would be today if every Christian was used by the Holy Spirit to pray out the Father's will in the earth?

Seeing Things Before They Happen

As a father, I can remember many times when the Holy Spirit would show me what Satan had planned against my family, and He would give me strategies to stop Satan's attacks.

One night I was lying in bed. My oldest son was in grade school at the time. We lived out in the country in South Georgia down a long dirt road. In a dream, I remember seeing him walking down the road over to his friend's house, carrying his bat and glove to hit a few rounds with the friend, who also went to our church.

About four boys were in a circle. One of the boys was swinging a bat round and round in circles. I saw the boy accidentally hit my son Joshua in the mouth, knocking out his front teeth. The dream was real. I prayed in the Spirit, bound the devil, and held the blood of Jesus over him, then rolled over and went back to sleep.

The next day I was coming home from the church in my pickup. I was driving slowly down our dirt road and passed Josh who had a bat on his shoulder and a glove in his hand. He was going over to his buddy's house to play. I waved at him and passed by. Then I remembered the dream I had the night before!

I slammed on my brakes, put the truck in reverse, and drove up next to him and said, "Get in!" Josh said, "What's the matter, Daddy?" I said, "Get in. You're not going over to Jerry's house today. I saw something bad happen to you and you're not going!" Josh looked at me with a puzzled look, but he said, "Okay," and we drove down the dirt road to our house.

Josh just hung around the house that afternoon. A few hours later the phone rang. It was our neighbors down the road who go to our church. Miss Jan said we needed to earnestly pray because the other neighbor kid just had his front teeth knocked out and the parents were taking him to the emergency room. That went a long way with my oldest son knowing that his daddy was there in the Spirit to protect him. How awesome are the things of God!

People who don't know how to grow will stay complacent and lethargic and will be powerless against the devil. It is more than telling someone, "Hold on just a little while, Brother!" Prophetic prayer enables us to remain calm in the midst of any storm and to hold fast to a spirit of faith in the midst of tribulation.

"Give Us This Day Our Daily Bread"

Can you remember when your prayer life consisted of a list? There is nothing wrong with writing things down and making your requests known to God, but there is a place in *proseuche* where we place a demand on the covenant. Jesus said, **"And all things, whatsoever ye shall ask in prayer, believing, ye shall receive"** (Matthew 21:22). The list I am talking about is, "Lord, by the way, I need a million dollars, so help me win that sweepstakes and I'll give You half. Amen."

Some of my relatives had an attitude that if you wanted something from God, then you had to keep nagging Him: "Hey, Lord, it's me again. I'm still waiting for You to do something with this buzzard of a husband You gave me!"

The Bible says in Isaiah 33:6, **"Wisdom and knowledge shall be the stability** [shock absorbers] **of thy times. . . ."** No matter what happens in the earth or around us, we can say of the Lord, "He is my refuge and my strong tower. In His name will I place my trust!" We may face the same potholes on the road that the world faces, but the difference is that God's wisdom absorbs roughness and turbulence so that peace rises up in our spirits through seasons of prayer and fasting.

No matter what happens anywhere on the earth, God's favor will bring us our my daily bread. What destroys the heathen will not destroy us. If we are laid off from work, the stock market falls, or there is a calamity in our nation, we will not lose hope. God will supply our provision if it has to come through a bird. God will bring direction if it has to come through a donkey.

What wipes out a religious man who prays will not change our attitude because we are in the secret place. The Lord wants to take care of us on a daily basis. Therefore, we must *proseuche* on a daily basis. Many Christians present their need without being in fellowship with God.

It's Time for a Heart Search

There is a place that the prophetic church will move into in these last days. Jesus said, **"Watch and pray** *[proseuche]* **. . ."** (Matthew 26:41), and **"Forgive us our**

debts, as we forgive our debtors" (Matthew 6:12). Some Christians do not want to spend time communing with God or in praise and worship because the presence of God convicts them of their sin, or a face comes up before them of someone they do not like. The Spirit of God shines a light in our closet and we get uncomfortable.

If we are going to move on with God into new heights of prayer, the Holy Spirit will not leave the dark areas alone that are within our hearts. The Psalmist David cried out, **"Search me, O God, and know my heart: try me, and know my thoughts: and see if there be any wicked way in me . . ."** (Psalm 139:23,24). To grow up into sonship, the Holy Spirit must be allowed to work in areas of our lives not yet surrendered to Him.

Spiritual Maturity

Romans 8:14 reads, **"For as many as are led by the Spirit of God, they are the sons of God."** The word "son" denotes one who has reached maturity, one who has his Father's heart and can work in partnership with Him in the earth. This word "son" translates in the Greek to the word *huios,* meaning one who progressed from babyhood to childhood and on to manhood.

The 70s TV show, "Sanford and Son," was about a father and his son in the junk business. Notice, the show was not "Sanford and Baby" or "Sanford and Boy." It was "Sanford and Son." Lamont was old enough to assist his father in the junk business.

Some of you may have seen business ads that read "Ward and Sons." There would not be many calls in response to your newspaper ad if it read, "Ward and

Babies." "Son" refers to someone who can carry weight and responsibility for their actions and is skillful enough to work in partnership with his father.

Later in this book, we will study out the Greek word *entunchano,* which translates as "intercession" in the New Testament. This book is titled *Prophetic Prayer to Sonship* for a reason.

Discerning the Spiritual Forecast

We must be taught the importance of prophetic prayers and being able to discern the spiritual forecast of what God is doing in the earth. I believe prayer warriors who know how to pray effectually will carry out "prayer assignments" in the next few years to even change the course of history.

During World War II, there was a man of prayer named Reese Howell. He and some mighty intercessors who were hooked to him in prayer actually prayed out the plan of the Holy Spirit by the Spirit of God within them. He began to pray that Hitler would divide his army into two different fronts. They spent much time in prayer and fasting over this and many hours in travail around the clock.

As they prayed out "the mind (plan) of the Spirit," Hitler made the biggest mistake when he turned on his ally, Russia, while he was totally engrossed on the European arena. History tells us that this was his military downfall. What a military strategy. The best military strategist in the universe is our Father God. Why do you think He is called "the Captain of the Host"?

Even in the earth today, God always intended that there would be prophets available to guide the king in decisions that would affect thousands and even millions of people. Are you willing to associate yourself with people who can hear specifically on what the terrorists are planning? What if the Lord wanted you to pray about the whereabouts of bin Laden? What if you had a vision that he is hiding in the Tora Bora Mountains in Afghanistan? What if you had a vision that he travels back and forth from the Tora Bora region into Northern Pakistan? Would you pray through?

What if you saw Al Qaeda planning an attack in the United States? What if you knew they were in strategic locations and had a plan to simultaneously try to sabotage our communications network in Cincinnati and the oil distribution in Houston? Can the Holy Spirit wake you up in the middle of the night to pray for our president and his protection?

In the Old Testament there was a prophet who knew the strategies and plans of the king while he was in his bed chamber. Can there be a prophet network that can alert the president before Satan strikes? Yes and Amen!

Prophets and prophetic people will speak with incredible accuracy in these last days, just like they did in the Old Testament. There are apostles and prophets in these last days who will carry the prophetic voice to kings and governments. You might not be called to the office of a prophet, but you can still be a part of a mighty army that will speak, "Thus saith the Lord" to every nation, tribe, and tongue. Several times in Revelation the Apostle John said, **"Hear what the Spirit saith unto the churches."**

Chapter Three

DO ALL THINGS WORK TOGETHER FOR GOOD?

In the last thirty years, I have heard Romans 8:28 quoted many times as a "catchall" for every calamity that happens which is unexplainable. Why do bad things happen to good people?

I have heard of horrific things like someone's house burning to the ground and losing all of their possessions, then some preacher says, "Well, all things work together for good."

What if a child dies in a car wreck and we are told to thank God for everything? Actually the Bible says, **"In every thing give thanks: for this is the will of God in Christ Jesus concerning you"** (1 Thessalonians 5:18). We are to thank God *in* every situation, but not *for* every situation.

In John 10:10 Jesus said, **"The thief cometh not, but for to steal, and to kill, and to destroy: I am come that they might have life, and that they might have it more abundantly."**

Those who are growing in sonship understand the true character of God. It is easy to pray to a loving God who has plans to bless us and make our way prosperous! Remember, God is a good God and the devil is a bad devil. They never swap jobs!

For years I have heard at funerals, especially when someone dies in an accident and is tragically taken out of the earth, "God needed another petunia in heaven." Or they will quote from the book of Job, **"The Lord gave, and the Lord hath taken away . . ."** (Job 1:21). Did anyone ever tell you that Job repented for saying that? Job said that and many other statements out of ignorance because he did not understand that it was Satan who robbed him of his children and stole all of his possessions. Later on at the end of the book of Job, he said to the Lord, **"Therefore have I uttered that I understood not . . ."** (Job 42:3).

I lost my father to cancer when he was only fifty-three years of age. It was hard, yet I knew the truth that it wasn't God's will for my father, at his young age, to go home to be with Jesus.

When I pray and lay hands on people for healing, it is so good to know that my heavenly Father wants those people healed even more than I do. If you have ever lost a loved one, you know the pain and suffering that are involved, and only the Comforter, the Holy Spirit, can bring a peace in the midst of the loss.

What we must know as Christians is that the Lord wants us to put a hedge of protection around our families that Satan cannot penetrate. As sons it is wonderful to know the power of the blood of Jesus, that when we pray and intercede, our prayers drive the forces of hell back!

Families who have lost everything in a hurricane or a tornado who don't know that God didn't cause the storm, many times will grow bitter against God and have a hard time trusting in their prayers. Romans 8:28 is not a "catchall" scripture for preachers or for Christians.

We need to clarify who Paul is referring to. He is talking to "sons." The Greek word for sons sometimes is *huios*. This scripture in Romans 8:28 is for those who are following the precepts in the entire eighth chapter of Romans. Romans 8:14 says, **"For as many as are led by the Spirit of God, they are the sons of God."**

Men and women of faith know Romans 8:26 that speaks of praying out the will of God and verse 27 that speaks of the mind of God. The power of praying in tongues and allowing that prayer to move into the realm of intercession by the Holy Spirit **"with groanings which cannot be uttered** [in articulate speech]" (v. 26).

Romans 8:28 works for sons who have been in *proseuche*. They are allowing the Holy Spirit to pray out the Father's will. They are listening to that still small voice as the Lord speaks to them and guides them in their daily affairs of life. Through *proseuche* they know the voice of God when He says, "Don't go to the park today alone," or, "Wait a half hour before you leave."

In the prayer time, that could be anytime during the day, sons know when the Holy Spirit will have them hold the blood of Jesus over their sons and daughters and learn to see things before they happen (Jeremiah 33:3).

The word "things" in Romans 8 means "the Word of God," not just any situation that comes your way. What this verse is telling us is, *God's Word works together for good to those who love God and who are called according to His purpose.* Christians have been taught or have heard that all circumstances will work together for good, *but it is the Word of God that will work together for your good.* Get the Word activated in your life. God can turn around what the devil has done to His sons.

It is time to bring our loved ones, our land, and our possessions out from under the curse! Live out the eighth chapter of Romans in your life and prosper in Jesus' name!

The Key to Understanding Suffering

If you have lost a child through some calamity or accident, or you know someone who has, it is important to minister the truth that God did not take their child, and even though the loss of their child is so great, they have a promise in the Word of God that as Christians, they will once again be united with that loved one in heaven.

When we pray, we need to learn to pray in line with the Word of God. We need to find scriptures in the Bible that promise what we are in need of. The Bible says in Psalm 91:16, **"With long life will I satisfy him, and shew him my salvation."** What an awesome promise!

Let's look at the promises in Jeremiah 29:11 and James 1:17.

> **For I know the thoughts that I think toward you, saith the Lord, thoughts of peace, and not of evil, to give you an expected end.**
>
> **Jeremiah 29:11**

> **Every good gift and every perfect gift is from above, and cometh down from the**

Father of lights, with whom is no variableness, neither shadow of turning.

James 1:17

When I pray, I pray to the God of miracles. I know that **"with God nothing shall be impossible"** (Luke 1:37).

Every person Jesus ever raised from the dead was a young person. It is the Father's will for us to live long lives. God is not a child abuser. He is not schizophrenic as some Christians would have you believe.

I remember when I was a child, one of my relatives said, "The Lord loves all of His children," and in the next breath declared, "God broke his leg to get his attention." I always grew up wondering if the Lord loved us so much, then why did He always allow bad things to happen to His children? If you can't trust your heavenly Father, then who can you trust? If sickness, disease, and hard times come into our lives to "make us better people," then the folks who are having the hardest time ought to know God the best. I used to think, *Ah, no thanks, God. I'll only bother You if I can't handle it on my own.* There are well-meaning people who only pray to God when they are in trouble or can't find their way out.

The Bible says in First John 3:8, **"For this purpose the Son of God was manifested, that he might destroy the works of the devil."** Did you get that? Jesus came to defeat the devil. As born-again believers, we are anointed in this life to **"lay hands on the sick, and they shall recover"** (Mark 16:18). We can pray effectually because we know that God's character is consistent and that He is full of love and is bestowing favor on us as a shield. Blessings in this life and true soul prosperity are available for those who are "called according to His purpose."

God Is for You!

We need to get a working knowledge of Romans 8:31, which says, **"If God be for us, who can be against us?"** When we pray, if we don't understand and truly believe that God did not take our child in crib death, then how can we love and put our trust totally in Him? Refuse to buy the lie that the devil has told you all these years. I speak to you to come up higher in Jesus' name!

I have been pastoring for over twenty years. I know how hard it is to lose a loved one to a terminal disease like cancer. My own father died of cancer in 1983, as I related earlier. What was so reassuring to me was that I knew that even though my dad died at fifty-three years of age, I knew that it was God's will that he would have lived a longer life. The spiritual authority in his life at that time told my dad, "It must be the will of God for the cancer to afflict you." Dad was actually healed of cancer in a healing service a few years before, when the cancer returned again to afflict him.

The Bible says that Satan comes and attacks us in seasons. So when my dad went back to his pastor when the symptoms started coming on his body again, his pastor told him, "This infirmity must be the will of God." It wasn't, but a few months later Dad was gone.

Why am I belaboring this point on suffering? I want you to get the revelation of the fact that it is God's will, when you pray, to see miraculous results of salvation and healing in your life and in others for whom you are praying.

It was very comfortable to know, as Frank Ward's son, that Dad chose to go home to be with Jesus. It was his choice to fight or to give in. He chose to give in. My mother, sister, and I released Dad to go home to be with the Lord.

When you are praying with those who are terminally ill, give them the opportunity to "choose to live"! Deuteronomy 30:19 says, **"I call heaven and earth to record this day against you, that I have set before you life and death, blessing and cursing: therefore choose life, that both thou and thy seed may live."** James 4:7,8 says, **"Resist the devil, and he will flee from you** [run in terror from you]. **Draw nigh to God, and he will draw nigh to you. . . ."**

My dad never had an opportunity to meet my wife and sons. I was ready to pray him up from the bed of affliction, but I could not override his will. Always remember to locate the person's faith. Dad was tired of fighting the good fight and wanted to go home. It was through praying *(proseuche),* through intercession *(entunchano),* and praying in the Holy Ghost that we knew it was time to commend my dad's spirit over to the Lord.

My mom, sister, and I did that one night in the very house I grew up in, standing by his bed of affliction. Just days after we had prayed and commended Dad's spirit over to the Lord, he went home. He went to sleep one night and woke up in the arms of his Savior! When we prayed, we had no bitterness at the Lord, but there was a peace in our hearts, knowing that Dad was no longer suffering.

If you have a loved one who is terminally ill and they are believing God for a miracle, stand in faith to see their deliverance. We have seen miracle after miracle of people getting off of their bed of affliction, even as I was preaching the Word! Fight the good fight of faith!

Some people have said, "Well, I prayed my heart out and they still died." If that has happened to you, listen to me. There are some things that happen that we cannot explain. The Bible says in Deuteronomy 29:29, **"The secret things belong unto the Lord. . . ."** We don't always know everything or why we pray *(proseuche)* and still do not see a person's deliverance from an infirmity.

Don't give up on God! Always know that it is God's will for that loved one to be raised up.

As sons, we learn in *proseuche* how to fight and how to contend for the faith, which is our covenant right. We must learn that the Word and the Spirit always agree. The voice of the Holy Spirit within our spirit will show us what to pray for (Romans 8:26,27).

Pastors, we need to teach our congregations about the different kinds of prayer. We need to know there are different rules governing prayer, and not just one kind of prayer is enough to lead a victorious life.

If you have ever been robbed by the enemy, stand up and demand that he (Satan) pay you back seven times. Where do I get that? From the Word of God – Proverbs 6:30,31!

Chapter Four

ENTUNCHANO — THE POWER OF INTERCESSION

We are about to embark on a study of the prayer of intercession based upon the Greek word *entunchano,* which means "the art of intercessory prayer" – to stand in the gap for a person, a group, or an entire nation. It is the Holy Spirit praying through your spirit.

The art of intercession is a very powerful weapon against the strategies of Satan. *Entunchano* requires a yielding to the Holy Spirit and a deep sensitivity of heart.

Proverbs 6:30,31 states:

> Men do not despise a thief, if he steal to satisfy his soul when he is hungry;
> But if he be found, he shall restore sevenfold; he shall give all the substance of his house.

Learn how to resist the devil when you stand praying and "make him flee" (James 4:7).

Romans 8:28 works for Christians (sons) who understand the power of *proseuche* – to listen and commune with their heavenly Father. It works for Christians (sons) who understand the power of *entunchano* – who stand in the gap by praying in the Spirit, with the Holy Spirit taking hold together with them to move the works of Satan.

As we develop our prayer lives as sons, we have revelation that the Lord's Prayer *(proseuche)* is the measuring rod of mercy we use on others, this being the same measuring rod Jesus uses on us.

As we are in communion with God in prayer, we have the Father's heart and His thinking on matters. We no longer will be so quick to "write off" people or ministers who have fallen, because we know the power of *deomai*. The power of supplication in the Spirit (Ephesians 6:18) or standing in the gap for those in prayer who we don't really feel deserve it.

"And lead us not into temptation, but deliver us from evil . . ." (Matthew 6:13). What is Jesus talking about? After you have done this type or degree of *proseuche*, you will begin to move more into the revelation. This is an awesome place to begin to see or perceive the strategies of the enemy before he attacks. This is a place where you can be used of God like never before. You are now learning to hear the prophetic voice of God. You are sensitive enough for the Holy Spirit to prompt you into a mode of prayer regardless of who or what is around you. How wonderful it is to know you are becoming an ambassador of prayer to change the natural course of lives and situations around you.

"No weapon [strategy] that is formed against thee shall prosper . . ." (Isaiah 54:17). This is when your sensitivity to the Holy Spirit through developing your prayer life gives you the ability for Him to steer you away from falling into the snares of the devil. Thank God for all the "prophecies" and "words" that we receive. That is a part of our growing in God, but for us to be able to receive daily direction from our heavenly Father is even more magnificent!

Start seeing every day as an opportunity for God to put you in "divine appointments" and to receive "divine assignments"! Has the Holy Spirit ever spoken to you? Have you ever heard the voice of God? Can you be sure that what you are hearing is from God? Yes, and again, I say, YES!

A Word from the Lord

Years ago when I was a young pastor in Southern Louisiana, I was in a ministers' conference with about two hundred ministers. A prophetess by the name of Billye Brim was ministering to us. Toward the end of her message, she came up to me and sat down in the pew right in front of me and began to prophesy concerning my future. She spoke to me concerning my call to the nations and what the Lord desired to accomplish in my ministry.

What was amazing to me is that when I was fifteen years old in Lake Worth, Florida, I was given almost the identical word from the Lord through another prophet, Bill Hammond. Both moved under a prophetic anointing and said some powerful words concerning my future in God. Being in the right place at the right time for a divine appointment enabled me to receive revelation and impartation that would change my life.

We can be led away from the snares and traps of the devil as we learn to follow the voice of God. Sometimes we need to look in the mirror and declare, *The Spirit of God has some major plans for me!* We can learn of these plans as we grow in sensitivity in hearing the voice of God concerning our prayer life.

Let the Holy Spirit Interrupt Your Plans

Several years ago, we had a missions trip planned to the nation of India. We were making plans to hold an open air crusade in Northern India (considered to be a missionaries' graveyard), yet the men I was to travel with never flinched when it came to "going into all the earth" as long as they knew it was a God-ordained trip.

One night while I was praying earnestly about the trip – praying for all the finances that were needed and also for protection on all who would be on the ministry team – I sensed the Lord did not want us to go on this particular trip. The more I prayed in the Spirit, I began to sense danger. I believe the Lord wanted to interrupt the "timing" of the trip and that we were to postpone it for a later date. We were ready in our hearts to "go into all the earth," yet I sensed strongly that there would be an assassination.

After a few more days of praying *(proseuche)*, I called the brethren who were going on the trip and told them what I was hearing in my spirit. Most of them decided to go anyhow due to all the inconvenience it would make after planning for an open air crusade. Usually it takes weeks, sometimes months, of preparation. Some of the ministry team went on the original dates we had planned to go.

Two weeks later, there was a tremendous political upheaval in India (at the same time I would have been there), thus forcing the missionary team to stay in their motel rooms because of the violence in the streets as a result of the assassination.

Thank God for the Holy Ghost! The missionary team was protected during this nation's upheaval, but still, thousands of dollars could have been saved if all of us had listened to the Holy Spirit concerning the dates. I had already told my congregation that I would not be going due to an assassination weeks before it happened.

A Hunger for the Supernatural

John G. Lake used to say, "There is a hunger in every man for the supernatural." The prophetic church will have a supernatural voice in these last days to speak to presidents and kings. This supernatural church will also have the means and resources to carry out each assignment for the advancing of the Kingdom of God in these last days. It is time for prophets to speak supernaturally to presidents concerning the future and concerning prophetic future events.

Through radio, television, and the printed page, this message will be carried to the ends of the earth. This is not a "wimpy" gospel being delivered by "wimpy" preachers! This voice is a "voice of victory"! This message is a "message of faith"! God will raise up men and women of faith who will speak to the nations concerning the future.

Ephesians 6:18 reads, **"Praying always with all [manner of] prayer** *(proseuche)* **and supplication** *(deomai)* **in the Spirit. . . ."** The Greek infers "all kinds of prayer." Then in verse 19, Paul goes on to say, "[Supplicate *(deomai)*] **for me that utterance may be given unto me, that I may open my mouth boldly, to make known the mystery** *[musterion]* **of the gospel.**"

We are going to see the prophetic church come together when we learn to *proseuche* together rather than bounce off of our senses. In a spirit of dominion and authority, we will do great exploits in these last days. A shaking is coming to the political arena and to our economy. Much frustration comes when you place energy into things that don't really matter.

When the word of the Lord comes forth to you, be quick to respond. I remember the word of the Lord came forth one Sunday morning while I was preaching and I said there would be a prominent minister in the area who would drop dead within three months and that people would be baffled by this occurrence. Many people asked why such a terrible thing could happen.

Almost three months to the day, in Lake Charles, Louisiana, one Sunday after the minister arrived home from church, he dropped dead in his own home. He was only fifty-one years old. The Lord had shared with me that this minister had refused to judge himself.

Judgment Falls

Years ago I was ministering to a large youth group in a Full Gospel church one night in Broken Arrow, Oklahoma. Young people were laying out all over the floor receiving the refreshing of the Spirit. Many of them had tears of joy and were drunk in the Spirit. Many received Holy Ghost laughter and were under the power of God. It was glorious.

While I was ministering, the pastor and two of his elders were standing in the back of the church watching us intently. They began to shake their heads in disbelief and signaled for me to shut the meeting down. They had never seen the refreshing or anyone drunk in the Spirit.

While the prophetic anointing was on me, I pointed at the three men and told them that if they didn't repent, their church would have a "padlock on the main door within thirty days." They laughed at me in disbelief. I respectfully prayed, finished the service, and went home. Twenty-eight days later that church of 350 people that had been in existence for over four years, was shut down.

We are in an hour where we can no longer "play church"! The day of the "wimpy preacher" is gone. As the prophets of old spoke to nations in the Old Testament, so shall it be in the last days. There is a new breed of ministers coming forth. Things are changing in the Spirit world. It is time to get on board and walk in the realm of the Spirit. We must hear and discern what the Holy Spirit is saying unto the churches.

What Is Prophetic Prayer to Sonship?

Sonship is a place in God that we attain by growing up spiritually. We grow from newborn babes as it says in the epistle to Peter; to children as it says in Ephesians; and then into sons as it is recorded in the book of Romans. **"For as many as are led by the Spirit of God, they are the sons of God"** (Romans 8:14).

Now, when we speak of "sons," I am not referring to the doctrine that was floating around fifty years ago called "Manifest Sonship." This doctrine was heretical with teaching that Satan himself would one day be restored to fellowship with God. This doctrine also taught that we would go through the Tribulation Period. These people would grow up into manhood and they themselves would defeat Satan and the Antichrist. This is false doctrine. This is *not* what I am referring to when I speak of sonship. Now that we have that cleared up, let's go into the revelation of what true sonship means, as described in the Word of God.

This book is all about developing our prayer life and bringing it to a higher level. There will always be extremes and abuses in every movement of God. Many great teachers of the faith have taught us concerning the need to grow up spiritually.

The spirit of prophetic prayer has everything to do with the hour we are living in. The Holy Spirit has chosen to reveal things to us right now because the end of the Church age is upon us.

For instance, we must understand that prayer for Israel's protection and well-being should be in the heart of every Christian. The Bible tells us to pray for the peace of Jerusalem. Presidential elections will be affected by candidates' political views of Israel.

I am instructed in the prophetic on how to share my studies with you concerning prophetic prayer to sonship. Those who want to work on cars will study manuals, watch films, and experience hands-on training about how to be a mechanic. You probably will never pick up a manual on rebuilding an engine if you don't like to get your hands dirty. Neither will there be any interest in the different types of prayer, nor the rules that govern them if you don't like to pray. There is progression to sonship, or maturity, by learning what God's Word has to say about the subject.

Thousands of people may read this book and say, "Oh, yeah, I've heard about that intercession stuff." Others may weep and shake under the power of God as they hear what the Spirit is saying to the churches. The carnal mind is always against what it does not understand. There is a big difference in the AM and FM radio frequencies. The late Brother Kenneth E. Hagin used to say that you get the message of faith after you have heard it a thousand times.

Chapter Five

AITEO — PLACING A DEMAND ON THE COVENANT

Matthew 7:7 says, **"Ask** *[aiteo]*, **and it shall be given you. . . ."** I like to compare learning to expand our prayer life to learning how to use the metric system.

Everywhere in the world, the metric system is used for weights and measures, except for the United States. Years ago the government started having the metric weight and measurements placed on liquid and food packages next to our standard American measurements. I remember learning to say "two liters" of Coke. It used to seem so strange. Now, using "liters" for Coke is a household term.

Forty years ago we had to develop a working knowledge of what a meter is. If you travel to Europe, their 80 kmph is not the same as our 80 mph. American vehicles now have smaller numbers on the speedometer for the metric system. Nuts and bolts of today very often come metric instead of SAE. Mechanics must have a working knowledge of which system to implement.

I use this analogy concerning our prayer lives. So many Christians are trying to use SAE when they need a metric tool for their nuts and bolts. We must develop a working knowledge of the different kinds of prayer available to us as Spirit-filled believers.

There are many connotations to "asking the Lord" for our prayers to be answered. Jesus did say, **"Ask, and it shall be given you . . ."** (Matthew 7:7).

What Does *Aiteo* Mean?

Aiteo means to place a loving demand on the covenant, based upon relationship. Every time you see the word "ask," it is the word *aiteo*. Because of some "religious" concepts we have concerning asking when we pray, we could interject the word "nag" or "whine" when we pray. You have probably been there before.

Can you remember when you prayed something like this: "Well, Lord, here I am again. I'm still waiting on You to do something with my husband. I asked You yesterday and our situation isn't any better."

People can take on the attitude that they will keep asking, and if you ask (nag) enough, then God will eventually hear you and answer your prayer. This is definitely the wrong attitude! Nagging God does not get Him to move faster.

There is nothing wrong with staying before the face of the Lord, but our attitude is based upon our relationship to keep on placing a demand on the covenant and you will receive. Prayer is a privilege when we understand *proseuche* (1 Thessalonians 5:17). *Aiteo* is based on a relationship with God.

Everything is being accelerated in the Spirit. Revelation on prayer is being quickened to the believer who is hungry for more of God. What took the last hundred years for the Church to walk in will take just a few years for us to learn before the Lord's return. This is the sovereign plan of God.

Faith: Our Course of Life

First John 5:4 states, **"For whatsoever is born of God overcometh the world** [system]**: and this is the victory that overcometh the world** [system]**, even our faith."** Whenever you see "faith" in Scriptures, it is referring to a course of life. We get the word "faith" from *pistos*. It means an elevated path or course of life. It is a predetermined highway. We are to contend for the faith. If we are to contend for the faith, then that must mean there is some resistance to keep us from it.

God has a plan for our lives. He also has a plan for His Church and for Israel. Jesus, being the Head of the Church, is the Author and Finisher (Developer) of our faith *(pistos)*.

First John 5:6-9 states:

> **This is he that came by water and blood, even Jesus Christ; not by water only, but by water and blood. And it is the Spirit that beareth witness, because the Spirit is truth.**
> **For there are three that bear record in heaven, the Father, the Word, and the Holy Ghost: and these three are one.**
> **And there are three that bear witness in earth, the Spirit, and the water, and the blood: and these three agree in one.**

If we receive the witness of men, the witness of God is greater: for this is the witness of God which he hath testified of his Son.
We have heard in many denominational churches that the water being referred to here is the water of baptism. Other scholars believe the water is referring to the "washing of the water of the Word." The word "water" here is the water of being born of a woman – the water in the placenta. If you are to be born again, you must be born of the water (from the womb) and of the Spirit. You cannot be born again if you are a disembodied spirit. You cannot be impregnated if you are a demon or an angel. You must be born of a woman to have full expression and legal right to be on this planet.

In John 10:1 Jesus said, **"Verily, verily, I say unto you, He that entereth not by the door into the sheepfold, but climbeth up some other way, the same is a thief and a robber."** Jesus entered into the door of humanity by being born of a woman. When He entered into humanity, He became the Shepherd of the sheep. He was also the door or port of entry for the sheep to have access to the heavenly Father.

This is why Jesus is the head of the Church. So entering into the door or being born of a woman gave Him the right to carry out the dominion in the earth as the second Adam, or the last Adam. This is why the devil could not understand how the Christ could come to the earth, because Satan could not understand why Jesus was able to operate in a spirit of dominion, when all the forefathers before Him had been controlled by their sinful nature.

The Father had a plan from the origin of time. He knew He would send His Son. He knew there would be an intercessor named Abraham with whom He could walk in covenant *(hesed)*. He also knew He would have a Church that would be like Jesus. Jesus has always referred to us as His bride. **"That he might present it to himself a glorious church, not having spot, or wrinkle, or any such thing; but that it should be holy and without blemish"** (Ephesians 5:27). Every time we look at the Church today, we see blemishes everywhere. We appear to be everything but spotless!

However, that is why we can look at the broader plan for things in the earth. We can see that the dispensation we are living in is coming to a close. Things are happening very quickly in the earth.

Let's look at First John 5:13-15:

> **These things have I written unto you that believe on the name of the Son of God; that ye may know that ye have eternal life, and that ye may believe on the name of the Son of God.**
>
> **And this is the confidence that we have in him, that, if we ask** *[aiteo - place a loving demand on the covenant]* **any thing according to his will, he heareth us:**
>
> **And if we know that he hear us, whatsoever we ask** *[aiteo]*, **we know we have the petitions that we desired of him.**

We can place a demand on the covenant by the Spirit of God within us. When we realize the power that God has given us through prophetic prayer, we can get excited. This is a depth of prayer through which we achieve.

Full Partnership with the Lord

James 5:7 states, **"Be patient therefore, brethren, unto the coming of the Lord. Behold, the husbandman waiteth for the precious fruit of the earth, and hath long patience for it, until he receive the early and latter rain."**

We are growing up into sonship so we can be trusted in this hour with the fullness of God's grace and anointing. True sons can carry their weight in the realm of the Spirit, being in full partnership with the Lord.

Mark 16:20 says, **"And they went forth, and preached every where, the Lord working with them, and confirming the word with signs following."** In our prayer lives in the past, it was all up to the Lord and what He could do. Now, it is time to decree in our prayer a thing to be established in the earth. We are nothing in ourselves, but in Christ we are complete.

James 5:13 reads, **"Is any among you afflicted? let him pray** *[proseuche]*. . . ." The word "afflicted" represents the initial attack of sickness or disease. **"Is any sick among you? let him call for the elders of the church . . ."** (v. 14). Affliction comes at the first sign of sickness or disease. The Bible tells us to pray *(proseuche)*. The word "sick" that follows it is when you progress from the initial attack of affliction and have not been able to move the infirmity by your own faith and prayer *(proseuche)*. This is when you need some backup or prayer assistance from those who can stand with you in faith. This is when you call for the elders of the church. The elders pray, anoint you with oil, and the *proseuche* of faith is spoken.

Most churchgoers do not start praying at the first sign of sniffling or the initial pain. We call the preacher to come pray. If you are the afflicted, you are to *proseuche* first!

If I am attacked, my response is to get in tune with God. Through prayer I can find out if I have let the hedge of protection down through sin, unforgiveness, or even strife. Was it something I said? Something I did?

James 3:16 states, **"For where envying and strife is, there is confusion and every evil work."** Or, is this "evil work" an illegal attack? We can bring this affliction on ourselves when we do not take care of our bodies. Not eating right, lack of sleep, or simply staying under prolonged stress. We can bring affliction upon ourselves because we broke spiritual laws. Whatever the case may be, if we will *proseuche* (Luke 11) with the steps Jesus told us, we will develop a spirit of wisdom on how to change what we are feeling in our bodies.

After praise, declaring the Kingdom promises, and checking our hearts for unforgiveness, we will come into the place of revelation. If we get out of the will of God, we can open ourselves up to affliction. Most folks want the pastor to be available to move the affliction for them. Prophetic people do soul-searching first – themselves!

James 5:14-15 states:

> **Is any sick among you? let him call for the elders of the church; and let them pray [*proseuche*] over him, anointing him with oil in the name of the Lord:**
> **And the prayer of faith shall save the sick, and the Lord shall raise him up; and if he hath committed sins, they shall be forgiven him.**

The elders and spiritual leadership are supposed to have an even greater anointing on their lives to pray. They will *proseuche* for you and help you through your infirmity. Prophetic prayer will require you to search your own heart.

Benefits of a Prophetic Prayer Life

James 5:16 states, **"Confess your faults one to another, and pray one for another, that ye may be healed. The effectual fervent prayer *[proseuche]* of a righteous man availeth much."** There is tremendous power available, and an incredible anointing is released when the righteous get fervent about *proseuche*.

Jesus was alone praying and His disciples were with Him. Mothers can be alone praying and their children be around them. You can be alone praying when fellow employees or your boss are still around you. There is *proseuche* you can do without ceasing. It makes absolutely no difference where you are.

There are times in *proseuche* where we are just to listen. Sometimes we get so tired, the only time we pray is with a long list instead of taking enough time to truly listen. Answered prayer and a powerful prayer life are not entirely up to God. The Holy Spirit reveals the plan.

Ephesians 3:2-4 states:

> **If ye have heard of the dispensation of the grace of God which is given me to you-ward:**
> **How that by revelation he made known unto me the mystery; (as I wrote afore in few words,**
> **Whereby, when ye read, ye may understand my knowledge in the mystery of**

Christ). [This means you have to become a part of this before you can fully understand.]

You can become a member of the Body of Christ and find out what this mystery is all about and find out about your membership benefits.

This reminds me of a story about a young man who bought a ticket on an ocean liner in the 1950s. He brought his peanut butter and crackers with him to eat on the five-day cruise to Europe. Every day he would walk the decks and smell the aroma of fine cuisine. He would see people eating to their hearts' content through the windows of the fine restaurants on the ship.

After the ship docked in England, he told the porter that the next time he wished to purchase a ticket that allowed him to eat all the fine full-course meals. The porter looked at him with astonishment, and said, "Sir, didn't they tell you that your ticket allowed you to eat at any restaurant or pub three times a day for the duration of your trip?"

I believe when we finally get to heaven, so many well-meaning Christians will say, "Lord, I had no idea I could have been so blessed and healed and prosperous on the earth. I just didn't know!" The Prophet Hosea, speaking by the Spirit of the Lord, basically said the same thing: **"My people are destroyed for lack of knowledge . . ."** (Hosea 4:6).

The Secrets of the Mystery

"Praying always with all prayer and supplication in the Spirit, and watching thereunto with all perseverance and supplication for all saints" (Ephesians 6:18). Paul is basically saying, *"Proseuche,* communing with God through the different types of prayer. The supplication, perseverance, and endurance for 'the saints and for me.'"

In verse 19 Paul goes on to say, **"And for me, that utterance may be given unto me, that I may open my mouth boldly, to make known the mystery of the gospel."** The word "mystery" in the Greek is *musterion*. In today's vernacular it would also be included in our word "fraternity."

There are many types of fraternities in the New Testament. When Jesus was on the scene, there was a fraternity called the "Magi." Today we think of universities and colleges where students join a group that has a certain cause, some having secrets about them. The Masons are a type of fraternity. They have certain sign language, things they say, and rituals that only Masons understand.

As Christians, when we talk about intercession or standing in the gap or believing God, most people do not understand what we are talking about. To understand what is available for us as Christians, we need to become a member. We join up when we receive Jesus Christ as Lord and Savior of our lives. There are definitely benefits in becoming a member of the Body of Christ. As a member you are entitled to:

A. Eternal life (forgiveness of sins).

    1. The promise of your whole household being saved.

    2. To live forever with the Lord in heaven.

B. To have a relationship with the one true God.

C. Soundness of mind, including freedom from fear.

1. The ability to understand the holy Scriptures.

D. Divine health, including divine healing for others.

E. Favor with God and man (abundant life).

F. Prosperity (riches and honor, being able to sow into every good work).
   1. Leaving an inheritance to your children's children.
   2. That everything we put our hands to would prosper.

G. Angelic protection.
   1. We will not be caught "off guard" concerning Satan's devices (plans).

H. The ability to hear the voice of God.

I. Answers to your prayers (when you pray in line with God's Word).

J. The ability to know what your purpose is here on the earth.

K. The baptism of the Holy Ghost (and the anointing of the gifts of the Holy Spirit).

This is by no means an exhaustive list, but it will help you to understand the "mystery."

Are you aware of what your membership in the Body of Christ is all about? Not only has Jesus made a way for us to go to heaven, but He provided health, favor, peace, soundness of mind, angelic protection, and prosperity for us.

Many Christians put off their victory to the "sweet by and by." "Victory will be on the other side. Just go through this life as a pilgrim." No! This ticket has already been bought and paid for by the stripes and blood of Jesus.

Our prayer lives can change the scenery we do not like in our lives. Ephesians 3:4-5 says:

Whereby, when ye read, ye may understand my knowledge in the mystery of Christ Which in other ages was not made known unto the sons of men, as it is now revealed unto his holy apostles and prophets by the Spirit.

Some of the prophetic revelation in these last days is going to come from the apostolic and prophetic ministries. If you do not know an apostle or a prophet, then you will miss out on pertinent information that is vital for you to walk victoriously in the next few years. It is hard to receive the apostolic and prophetic ministries if you are in a church that does not believe in them.

The Lord has apostles and prophets all over the earth. Are you willing to break out of your tradition to go sit under one?

There is revelation coming forth in the next few years that will literally cause God's people to rise and do great exploits, while cities and nations come to God before the Lord's return. Right now the Lord is giving prayer assignments to His people who are listening. People and ministries are being strategically positioned by God.

Somewhere there is an intercessor walking the streets praying earnestly and every place he or she steps is being claimed for the Kingdom of God. Somewhere in the earth, even as you read this book, there is a regiment of those who are standing in the gap for presidents and kings and for Israel. They are praying out and birthing the plan of God by yielding themselves to the Holy Spirit.

Demonstrating the Manifold Wisdom of God

Let's look at Ephesians 3:6-15:

> That the Gentiles should be fellowheirs, and of the same body, and partakers of his promise in Christ by the gospel:
> Whereof I was made a minister, according to the gift of the grace of God given unto me by the effectual working of his power.
> Unto me, who am less than the least of all saints, is this grace given, that I should preach among the Gentiles the unsearchable riches of Christ;
> And to make all men see what is the fellowship of the mystery, which from the beginning of the world hath been hid in God, who created all things by Jesus Christ:
> To the intent that now unto the principalities and powers in heavenly places might be known by the church the manifold wisdom of God,
> According to the eternal purpose which he purposed in Christ Jesus our Lord:
> In whom we have boldness and access with confidence by the faith of him.
> Wherefore I desire that ye faint not at my tribulations for you, which is your glory.

> **For this cause I bow my knees unto the Father of our Lord Jesus Christ,**
> **Of whom the whole family in heaven and earth is named.**

What can we learn from these verses? In these last days, the principalities and powers will know that time in this dispensation is coming to a close, just by looking at the Church. The demon powers in the earth know that their eminent doom of defeat and judgment is near because they can see the glory of God on the bride of Christ growing stronger and stronger. The Bible says they can see the **"manifold wisdom of God"** (Ephesians 3:10) coming forth on the end-time Church.

Where there is manifold tribulation on every side, there is manifold wisdom available for the end-time Christians. Those who choose to be on the Lord's side and walk under the counsel of His Word will do great exploits in demonstrating the wisdom of God.

Ask yourself these questions: Am I receiving answers to my prayers? Am I satisfied with a "hit and miss" prayer life? Or am I ready to get fine-tuned by the Holy Spirit within me? Is my prayer life shaping my future?

When we begin to understand the mystery, we can begin to walk in our Kingdom rights of what Jesus paid for through His death, burial, and resurrection. Understanding the mystery will enable you to transform your prayer life.

James 1:5 says, **"If any of you lack wisdom** *[sophia]*, **let him ask** *[aiteo]* **of God. . . ."** "Wisdom" is a powerful word in the Greek language. It means a broader scope of what is happening behind the scenes.

As we allow the Holy Spirit in us to aid us in our prayer life, we can expect to increase in a Spirit of wisdom to know how to deal with every situation that comes to us. If we choose to walk in a Spirit of wisdom, we can look at any crisis or problem that comes our way through a different set of eyes and ears than the world looks through. If we are having problems in our relationship with our spouse, our prayer life can be enhanced through a Spirit of wisdom that will enable us to have a broader scope of what's happening behind the scenes.

If our children are rebelling and we don't know what to do, we can have a broader scope of what's happening behind the scenes and see what the root source is that we need to bind or loose. We are able to perceive in our spirit the cause of the rebellion and deal with it in the Spirit.

Pastor James said if we lack a broader scope of what's happening behind the scenes, we are to place a loving demand upon the covenant we have with God.

For this cause I bow my knees unto the Father of our Lord Jesus Christ,
Of whom the whole family in heaven and earth is named.
Ephesians 3:14-15

Notice, you have family in heaven and in earth – in two different places. The book of Revelation says there is going to be a time when we are all transferred out (Revelation 4). Right now, we have family in the "cloud of witnesses" (Hebrews 12:1), or better translated, in the "grandstands of heaven." The folks in heaven may not know when you bought a new car or changed your job, but they are aware of spiritual advances you are making.

Greater Revelation

God wants to grant unto you according to His riches in glory an anointing of revelation that He has for you to walk in today that literally was hidden from other dispensations. How exciting it is that God wants to use us as prayer warriors to stop evil in the earth as we take our place as intercessors in these last days.

That he would grant you, according to the riches of his glory, to be strengthened with might by his Spirit in the inner man;

That Christ may dwell in your hearts by faith; that ye, being rooted and grounded in love,

May be able to comprehend with all saints what is the breadth [the storehouse of God's Word]. . . .

Ephesians 3:16-18

Paul said in Acts 20:20, **"I kept back nothing that was profitable unto you. . . ."** Paul said that when it came to giving revelation through his apostolic office, he did not hold back anything. The Greek language denotes an unfurling of the sails on a boat.

Acts 20:27 states, **"I have not shunned to declare unto you all the counsel of God."** If you take this teaching to heart, you can come up higher in your prayer life in Jesus' name. There is a buffet ready for those who are hungry and thirsty for God.

The next word we'll look at from Ephesians 3:18 is "length." "Length" is defined as time orientation. If ever there has been a time that we need to understand the hour we are living in, it is today. Most of the Body of Christ are sleeping concerning the prophetic hour we are in. The world system is demanding more and more of our time. Time is an enemy until we come into fellowship with the Holy Spirit.

There is a mighty harvest of souls to be reached before the Lord comes back. We have not seen the former and latter rain come together yet. We have not seen the restoration of the fivefold ministry yet. We have not seen the Church open up all of her gifts that will bring her into her finest hour. The glory shall be revealed upon the Bride of Christ. We have not seen the gifts of the Holy Spirit in operation like we will in the next few years.

Chapter Six

WHAT TIME IS IT?

Is your "spiritual clock" in sync with the Father's clock? Do you know what hour it is in the Church age?

I might be involved in this world system eight, ten, or twelve hours a day, but I know that ultimately my help comes from the Lord.

Remember, we do not have to pray. We get to pray! Will you pray because you want to fellowship with the Lord or because some calamity or judgment brings you to your knees? If you will fellowship with God, it will not take eighty hours a week to make ends meet. God intends for us to have time with Him, our spouse, our children, and our church.

I refuse to be burned out on the world system when God's favor can do in a few minutes what would take us a lifetime of self-effort. The world system is destined to collapse anyway. I might work in the world system because God said He would bless what I put my hands to. Ultimately, when I pray, "Lord, bless me this day," He will.

Think big in a small place. God wants to bless you. You are part of the Abrahamic covenant. The breadth, length, depth, and height of Ephesians 3:18 means:

- Breadth   The storehouse of God's Word.
- Length   Time orientation.
- Depth   Our relationship with others.
- Height   Our relationship with God.

This kind of love that we are to comprehend is the kind that will cause us to pray for the unlovely and pray for the lost who are dying in their sins. This love casts out all fear and insecurity.

Ephesians 3:20 states, **"Now unto him that is able to do exceeding abundantly above all that we ask or think, according to the power that worketh in us."** God wants to bless His people abundantly above what we can ask [place a demand on the covenant] or think. What time is it? It is time for the windows of heaven to be opened and God's blessing to be poured out on you with a blessing bigger than you can even think. That's big!

We can expand our thinking into the breadth of God in every area of our lives. Get rid of your "pea-brained" thinking. We will lend and not borrow. We will leave an inheritance to our children's children.

Prophetic Prayer and the Harvest

I want to see entire cities come to the Lord. There is a Church triumphant coming forth that is militant, radical, and will not take "no" for an answer. We will see a mighty harvest.

> The harvest truly is plenteous, but the labourers are few;
> Pray *[proseuche]* ye therefore the Lord of the harvest, that he will send forth labourers into his harvest.
>
> **Matthew 9:37-38**

Skilled men and women will be sent into the harvest; sons who are skillful in the Word and in their prayer lives will reach the lost.

The anointing will slap you on your head sometimes. We need a prophetic word to shake us up and get us out of our comfort zones. Prophets are not just to rub your little head and tell you how wonderful you are. It is time to wake up. The prophetic word will be in demonstration and power. We will see the Bride of Christ respond to His Word.

The more we receive, the more that is required of us. That is why there is a stronger judgment on teachers. To know the reason why many Christians are in the shape they are in, listen to what they hear every week at church.

> **Not unto him that is able to do exceeding abundantly above all that we ask or think, according to the power that worketh in us,**
> **Unto him be glory in the church by Christ Jesus throughout all ages** [dispensations], **world without end. Amen.**
>
> **Ephesians 3:20-21**

Ephesians 4:1-2 states:

> **I therefore, the prisoner of the Lord, beseech you that ye walk worthy of the vocation wherewith ye are called,**

With all lowliness and meekness, with longsuffering, forbearing one another in love.

Powerful words! Stay teachable. In that strong love, we are secure in what God has called us to do. This is not the "sloppy agape" of the Charismatic Movement that rapidly wanted to comfort everyone.

Stand your ground in prophetic prayer for your mate and children who may seem like they do not want to go on with God.

Remember Joshua's declaration? **"As for me and my house, we will serve the Lord"** (Joshua 24:15).

In lowliness and meekness of heart, we can have an attitude of submission and humility, yielding to the Holy Spirit.

Are we experiencing pain for "the Word's sake"? Or is it because we shot ourselves in the foot? Are we experiencing pain because of our own stupidity, or for the sake of the gospel? Thank God for believers who will supplicate for us when we are going through hard places.

The carnal mind will cause pastors and ministries to compete for each other's sheep. The carnal mind will rejoice when another pastor falls into sin and the sheep join his flock. The carnal mind will rejoice when ministries kill their wounded instead of restoring them back to the love of Christ. When we operate in a wrong spirit, we crush people with our words.

Keep a servant's heart. The Holy Spirit knows where you live. Get in the breadth, length, depth, and height of God's will. Scientists believe there are actually eleven different dimensions that are in the law of physics. Most of us are limited to three. When we start walking in the glory of God, we can walk beyond the three dimensions and into what Adam walked in before the fall. This will be restored when we receive our glorified bodies.

Until then, get into the realms of prayer that are available to you through prophetic prayer. The result will be a lifestyle of overcoming faith and power that will demonstrate to the world the God-kind of life that will draw many sinners into the Kingdom of God!

A Sinner's Prayer

To Receive Jesus as Your Savior and Lord

Father, in Romans 10:9-10 You said, **"If thou shalt confess with thy mouth the Lord Jesus, and shalt believe in thine heart that God hath raised him from the dead, thou shalt be saved. For with the heart man believeth unto righteousness; and with the mouth confession is made unto salvation."**

Father, I believe in my heart that Jesus Christ is Your Son and that He was crucified, buried, and resurrected to pay the price in full so I can live victoriously over sin, sickness, poverty (both spiritual and natural), and spiritual death.

Jesus, I confess You as my Savior and Lord. Thank You that in You I am saved. I now become a new creation and I become righteous in You. Old things have passed away and all things become new (see 2 Corinthians 5:17,21).

Thank You, Lord Jesus, for empowering me with Your Spirit so I can live an overcoming, abundant life and become a bold witness of You!

Today my new life begins in You, Lord Jesus. Thank You!

_____
Signature

_____
Date

About the Author

David and Vonda Ward have been involved in singing, teaching, and prophetic ministry since 1982. They have helped pioneer several churches in the southern region of the United States and are founders of New Creation Missions International.

The Ward's ministry has carried them to 18 countries preaching the Good News of Jesus Christ.

N.C.M.I. has outreaches throughout the world including Medical Missions to Central America and to the Chernobyl children in the Ukraine delivering over 1.2 million dollars worth of humanitarian aid to the region.

With a unique teaching ability, Dave Ward has held prophetic conferences and Pastors' seminars worldwide teaching people with hungry hearts the whole counsel of the Word of God.

David and Vonda Ward currently pastor Legacy Family Church and World Outreach Center in Morris, Oklahoma.

For other books, tapes, or more
information concerning
David and Vonda Ward's Ministry, write:

New Creation Missions International
P. O. Box 596
Wagoner, Oklahoma 74467

Or visit:

www.ncmidave.com